108 Zen Parables and Stories

Contents

II   THE ART OF ZEN LIVING

III   THE ART OF ZEN DYING

Introduction

The origins of Zen Buddhism trace back to the late fifth century when a humble monk named Bodhidharma brought the teachings of Mahayana Buddhism to China from India. In China, these teachings combined with Taoism and formed the basis for what later became known as Chan or Zen Buddhism. Zen's golden age began with the Sixth Patriarch, Huineng (638-713) and ended with the persecution of Buddhism in China in the middle of the ninth century. During this time, Zen Buddhism developed its own form of expression. While traditional Buddhism emphasized sutras and scholastic treatises, Zen Buddhism focused on direct experience over doctrine. Attempting to capture this direct experience, the followers of Zen Buddhism assiduously compiled records of the actual sayings, known as koans (*public records*), of its prominent leaders or Zen masters. Some koans were in the form of questions or challenges to test the students' understanding of Zen, others intertwined with local legends and fables to become inventive stories and often a source of inspiration, direction and comfort for those in need of guidance.

So what can these Zen stories do for us? Contemporary Western culture often divides every matter through intellectual perception into good or bad, right or wrong. Zen Buddhism teaches us that this continuous judgement is deeply rooted in our sensory interpretation and diverts us further from the life of harmony and peace, the life in which oneness can be attained.

Dealing with the universal wisdom that transcends ordinary knowledge, Zen stories are meant to point out the simplicity of life and how duality must be transcended. And for a curious mind, they attempt to demonstrate how intellectual reasoning is futile to solve the questions of Zen masters, and how only through an understanding of the realm of non-attachment the dimension deeper than the world of the five senses could be perceived.

The traditional Zen stories and parables collected in this book were meant to serve this exact purpose — to be a silent companion waiting at one's elbow, ready to shed light. Each story, no matter how short and simple, holds the key to a resolution of timeless questions. As we read and solve these koans, story after story, we allow our true Buddha nature to free up from any obstructed perceptions of a fragmented mind and to flow in unison with the river of the universe.

May these stories bring you a gift of peace, joy and unshakable inner freedom.

I

THE ART OF ZEN TEACHING

"Not twice this day
Inch time foot gem.
This day will not come again.
Each minute is worth a priceless gem."

- poem by Takuan, a famous Zen master

EVERY MINUTE

~ഄളക~

After ten years of apprenticeship, Tenno achieved the rank of Zen teacher. One rainy day, he went to visit the famous master Nan-in. When he walked in, the master greeted him with a question, "Did you leave your wooden clogs and umbrella on the porch?"

"Yes," Tenno replied.

"Tell me," the master continued, "did you place your umbrella to the left of your shoes or to the right?"

Tenno, confused, had no instant answer. He realized that he had not yet attained full awareness. So he became Nan-in's student and studied under him for six more years.

Two

EVERYTHING WILL PASS

A student went to his master and said, "My meditation is so horrible! I feel so distracted, and my legs ache. Also, I'm constantly falling asleep!"

"It will pass," the master replied casually.

A week later, the student returned to his teacher and exclaimed, "My meditation is so wonderful! I feel so aware, so peaceful and so alive!"

"It will pass," the master replied casually.

Three

THE TREASURE HOUSE

One monk visited the great master Baso in China. Baso asked, "What do you seek?"

"Enlightenment," replied the monk.

"You have your own treasure house. So why do you search outside?" Baso asked.

"Where is my treasure house?" the monk inquired.

The master answered, "What you are asking is your treasure house."

Four

EMPTY MIND

A student once asked a great Zen master named Joshu, "If I haven't anything in my mind, what shall I do?"

"Throw it out," the master replied.

The student wondered, "But if there isn't anything, how can I throw it out?"

"Well," said Joshu, "then carry it out."

Five

EVERYTHING IS FINE

One Zen master, when someone asked him how he was doing, always replied that he was fine. Eventually, one of his students asked, "Teacher, how is it possible that you are always doing so well? Don't you ever have a bad mood?"

"Of course I do," the master responded, "But when I'm in a good mood, everything is fine. And when I'm in a bad mood, everything is fine too."

Six

CHOOSING A MASTER

Two masters were invited to visit a nobleman who wanted to learn more about Zen practice. Upon arriving, the first master said to the nobleman, "You are skilled and wise by nature and certainly have an inborn talent to learn Zen."

"Nonsense," the second master responded. "He may be of a noble origin, but he knows nothing of Zen. Why do you flatter him?"

With these remarks, the nobleman, without any hesitation, decided to build a temple for the second teacher and study Zen with him.

Seven

BACK TO SAFETY

The district governor named Hakurakuten heard of this famous Zen monk who lived on a tree and decided to visit him one day. Seeing the monk perched high up in the tree, the governor said, "Living on the tree is quite dangerous. You might fall at any moment. So why don't you live on the ground?"

The monk replied, "Is it safe down there on the earth?"

Eight

THE SOUND OF ONE HAND

The master of Kennin temple, Mokurai, Silent Thunder, had a little protege named Toyo who was only twelve years old. Toyo saw the older disciples visit the master's room each morning and evening to receive instruction and koans to stop mind-wandering.

Toyo wished to receive a koan also.

"Wait a while," said Mokurai. "You are too young."

But the child insisted, so the teacher finally consented. In the evening, little Toyo went to the master's room at the proper time, bowed and listened respectfully.

"You can hear the sound of two hands when they clap together," said Mokurai. "Now show me the sound of one hand."

Toyo bowed again and went to his room to consider this problem. From his window, he could hear the melodies of the local musicians. "Ah, I have it!" he proclaimed.

The next evening, when his teacher asked him to illustrate the sound of one hand, Toyo began to play the melodies we heard.

"No, no," said Mokurai. "That is not the sound of one hand. You've not got it at all."

Thinking that such music might interrupt, Toyo moved his abode to a quiet place. He meditated again. "What can the sound of one hand be?" He happened to hear some water dripping. "I have it," imagined Toyo.

When he next appeared before his teacher, he imitated dripping water.

"What is that?" asked Mokurai. "That is not the sound of one hand. Try again."

In vain Toyo meditated to hear the sound of one hand. He heard the sighing of the wind. But that sound was also rejected. Just as the cry of an owl. More than ten times Toyo visited Mokurai with different sounds. All were wrong. For almost a year he pondered what the sound of one hand might be. At last Toyo entered true meditation and transcended all sounds. At that instance, he realized the sound of one hand.

Nine

WHO KNOWS?

One emperor, a devout Buddhist, invited a great Zen master to the palace to ask him questions about Buddhism.

"What is the highest truth of the holy Buddhist doctrine?" the emperor inquired.

"Vast emptiness… and not a trace of holiness," the master replied.

"If there is no holiness," the emperor said, "then who or what are you?"

"I do not know," the master replied.

Ten

COUNTING LEAVES

Once a great master was sitting in a forest under a large tree when a well-versed scholar came up to him and asked, "People said that you are a great teacher. Have you taught everything that you know?"

The master took a few dry leaves and replied, "How many leaves have I got in my hand? Are they more than the number of dry leaves in this forest?"

The philosopher looked at the forest full of trees and said, "How could you have more leaves in your hand? You have only a few, a dozen at the most, and there are millions of leaves in this forest."

And the master replied, "Just so, that which I taught is like the few leaves in my hand. And that which I have not taught is like the dry leaves in this forest."

The scholar then queried, "Why have you not taught everything?"

The master said, "Because it will not help you. Not everything can be said; some knowledge has to be experienced."

Eleven

ASKING QUESTIONS

Once a young man with an inquisitive mind asked the Buddha yet another question. The Buddha listened to him carefully and replied, "I will give you the answer you are looking for, but first, you need to wait for one year. This is my condition."

Hearing this, Ananda, the Buddha's attendant, started laughing.

"Why are you laughing?" the young man asked Ananda.

"I am laughing because a year ago the Teacher told me the same thing: 'Wait one year in silence, seize the uncontrollable thoughts, then ask me again.' If you really want to ask, ask now."

"This is my condition," the Buddha repeated, "If you ask again in one year, I will answer."

After exactly one year had passed, the Buddha asked the young man, "Do you want to ask me anything?"

"O Teacher! I waited for a year in silence, seizing the uncontrollable thoughts. Now I understand why honorable Ananda was laughing. How would I ask anything if there were no more questions left in my head! When thoughts were gone, so were the questions."

Twelve

A QUICK LESSON

Once a philosopher, a true seeker, asked the Buddha, "Without words, without silence, will you tell me the truth?"

The Buddha sat quietly. The philosopher bowed in gratitude and said, "I have now cleared away my delusions and entered the true path."

After the man had gone, Ananda, the Buddha's attendant, asked what that philosopher had attained.

The Buddha commented, "A good horse runs even at the shadow of the whip."

Thirteen

DIFFERENT INSTRUCTIONS

Once a famous Zen master received a disciple from another monastery and asked him, "How does your teacher instruct you?"

"My teacher instructs me to shut my eyes and see no evil thing; to cover my ears and hear no evil sound; to stop my mind and form no wrong ideas," the disciple replied.

"I do not ask you to shut your eyes," the Zen master responded, "but you do not see a thing. I do not ask you to cover your ears, but you do not hear a sound. I do not ask you to cease your mind, but you do not have any idea at all."

Fourteen

TRUE SELF

A troubled man approached Zen master and pleaded, "I feel lost, desperate because I don't know who I am. Please, Master, show me my true self!"

Yet, the master just looked away without responding. The man continued to beg, but still the master did not respond. Finally giving up in frustration, the man turned to leave. At that moment, the master called out to him by name.

"Yes!" the man said as he spun back around.

"There it is!" exclaimed the master.

Fifteen

WHO SHOULD BE THANKFUL?

One great Zen master had so many disciples that the quarters he was teaching in quickly became overcrowded. A wealthy merchant living nearby decided to donate five hundred pieces of gold called ryo toward constructing a more spacious premises for the monastery. This money he brought to the teacher.

The master said, "All right. I will take it."

The wealthy merchant gave the master the sack of gold. Since five hundred ryo was a lot of money, one could live a whole year on just three ryo, the merchant was expecting the teacher to thank him. However, when he didn't receive any gratitude, the merchant became dissatisfied and hinted, "In that sack are five hundred ryo."

"You told me that before," replied the master.

"Even for a very wealthy merchant, five hundred ryo is a lot of money," continued the merchant.

"Do you want me to thank you for it?" asked Zen master.

"I think you ought to," the merchant responded.

"Why should I?" inquired the teacher. "The giver should be thankful."

Sixteen

MAKING A MIRROR

The great Zen master Nanyue was the head of Prajna Temple, when a new young monk arrived. The young man worked hard, studying with the other monks and spending hour after hour sitting in the meditation hall. Carefully observing him, master Nanyue perceived that he was close to breaking through the web of illusion, and perceiving his true essence.

Thus, one afternoon Nanyue sat down beside the young monk and started polishing a roof tile.

The monk wondered why his master was doing that and asked, "Master, why on earth are you polishing a tile?"

"I'm trying to turn it into a mirror." In those days mirrors were made from pieces of metal polished to a high shine.

"How can polishing possibly make a piece of tile into a mirror? No matter how much you polish it, clay can't shine forth."

"And how can crossing your legs and sitting down make you a Buddha?"

responded Nanyue.

The young man was stunned. Almost forgetting to breathe, he asked Nanyue, "Then what should I do?"

"If an ox cart won't move, do you hit the cart or do you hit the ox?"

At that moment, the monk became enlightened.

Seventeen

A STRANGE TURTLE

A student saw a turtle in the garden of a Zen's monastery and asked his master, "All beings cover their bones with flesh and skin. Why does this being cover its flesh and skin with bones?

The master took off one of his sandals and covered the turtle with it.

Eighteen

WHAT'S YOUR AGE?

One boy asked a very old monk about his age.

The old monk replied, "I am four years old."

The child exclaimed, "How could that be? Your face is covered in wrinkles and your hair is completely white. How could you be four years old?"

"I am indeed only four years old. All my life I cared about myself and lived only for myself. Four years ago I understood how to see the true essence of human nature. At that moment my life became meaningful and only since then I experienced true peace and true calmness. That is why I am four years old - I only truly lived for four years," the monk replied.

Nineteen

CHASING TWO RABBITS

A martial arts student approached his teacher with a question, "I'd like to improve my knowledge of the martial arts. Would you mind if I also study with another teacher to learn another style?"

"The hunter who chases two rabbits," answered the master, "catches neither one."

Twenty

THE ARCHER

After winning several archery contests, the young and rather boastful champion challenged a Zen master who was renowned for his skill as an archer. The young man demonstrated remarkable technical proficiency when he hit a distant bull's eye on his first try, and then split that arrow with his second shot.

"There," the archer said to the old master, "see if you can match that!"

Undisturbed, the master did not draw his bow, but rather motioned for the young archer to follow him up the mountain. Curious about the master's intentions, the champion followed him high into the mountain until they reached a deep chasm spanned by a rather flimsy and shaky log. Calmly stepping out onto the middle of the unsteady and certainly perilous bridge, the old master picked a far away tree as a target, drew his bow, and fired a clean, direct hit.

"Now it is your turn," said the old man gracefully stepping back onto the safe ground. Staring with terror into the seemingly bottomless and beckoning abyss, the young man could not force himself to step out onto the log, no less

26

shoot at a target.

"You have much skill with your bow," the master concluded, "but little skill with the mind that lets loose the shot."

Twenty-One

WHAT IS EGOTISM?

The Prime Minister of the Tang Dynasty was a national hero for his success as both a statesman and military leader. But despite his fame, power, and wealth, he considered himself a humble and devout Buddhist. One day, during his usual visit, the Prime Minister asked the master, "O Teacher, what is egotism according to Buddhism?"

The master's face turned red, and in a very condescending and insulting tone of voice, he shot back, "What kind of stupid question is that!?"

The Prime Minister was shocked by this unexpected response and immediately became sullen and angry. The Zen master then smiled and said, "THIS is egotism."

Twenty-Two

TEA COMBAT

A master of the tea ceremony once accidentally slighted a soldier. He quickly apologized, but the rather impetuous soldier demanded that the matter be settled in a sword duel. The tea master, who had no experience with swords, asked the advice of a fellow Zen master who did possess such skill. As he was served by his friend, the Zen swordsman could not help but notice how the tea master performed his art with perfect concentration and tranquillity.

"Tomorrow," the Zen swordsman said, "when you duel the soldier, hold your weapon above your head, as if ready to strike and face him with the same concentration and tranquillity with which you perform the tea ceremony."

The next day, at the appointed time and place for the duel, the tea master followed this advice. The soldier, readying himself to strike, stared for a long time into the fully attentive but calm face of the tea master. Finally, the soldier lowered his sword, apologized for his arrogance, and left without a blow being struck.

Twenty-Three

ALL BY YOURSELF

When one great Zen master became renowned for his spiritual practice, many people started coming to his temple to seek the master's guidance. More visitors led to more meals to prepare, ceremonies to conduct, and guests to look after. The temple where the master was living became very busy and not as quiet as it was before.

One student, a young monk, came to see the master and said, "Master, life here is so crowded and busy. It's really interfering with my spiritual practice. With your permission, I'd like to go somewhere deep in the mountains and find a quiet place where I can practice by myself."

The master studied his student for a moment and then answered, "Really? If that's what you want to do, go ahead. There's just one thing though. When you're hungry, don't eat anything that was harvested or prepared by others. Don't accept clothes from other people. If you can do all of these, you have my permission to go and practice by yourself."

The student just sat there, stunned by the master's unexpected reply. As the young monk carefully thought about his teacher's words, he realized that the master was describing how the world functioned, that there was nothing in this world that wasn't supported by the help of every other thing. Everything in this world lives together, as one life, helping and being helped. The monk then saw that any person or situation was just another aspect of himself. Their heart was his heart, their behavior was his behavior, and their pain was his pain.

Twenty-Four

THE CAUSE OF ALL PROBLEMS

One Zen master decided to teach a lesson about the cause of all problems. He took a glass of water in his hand and asked his students, "How much do you think this glass weighs?"

"About 300 grams," the students answered.

"Indeed. What happens if I hold this glass for a few minutes?"

"Almost nothing will happen," responded the students.

"Indeed. And what if I hold this glass for an hour?" asked the master.

"Your hand will get tired."

"Indeed. And what if I hold this glass for a few hours?"

"Your arm will start to hurt."

"Indeed. And hat if I hold this glass for the whole day?"

"Your hand will become numb, and your arm may even become paralyzed," one of the students replied.

"Very good," the master continued, "but has the weight of this glass changed?"

"No," the students answered.

"Then where did the pain come from?" the master asked.

"From prolonged stress," the students answered.

"Now, what do I need to do to get rid of the pain?"

"Lower the glass," came the answer.

"The same happens with all of life's problems," the master concluded. "Keeping them in your head for a few minutes does not hurt. Yet, if you think about them for hours, you will start experiencing some pain. If you think about them all day long, they might paralyze your mind, and you will not be able to do anything else. To get rid of this pain, let the problems out of your head."

Twenty-Five

WISDOM OF THE WORLD

Once a man came to a famous Zen master and complained that he could not understand the wisdom of the world, no matter how he tried. And since he could understand the wisdom of the world, he started to doubt the wisdom of God. This caused a lot of confusion in him, therefore he came to ask for help. The master agreed to help this man but only if he would fulfill three requirements.

The first requirement was to sit on the shore and listen to the river singing. "This is the voice of God," said the master.

And so the man did. In the evening, however, when the monk asked if he understood the wisdom of the world, the man shook his head.

Then the monk told the man to look into the fire. "This is the dance of God," said the master.

And so the man did. In the evening, however, when the monk asked if he understood the wisdom of the world, the man shook his head. The earth and the air also did not tell the man anything about the wisdom of the world, for he did not discern their secrets.

The monk thought about and the next day he said, "Then look into yourself. All your doubts lurk in there."

And so the man did and, seeing in his soul the reflection of the whole universe, he finally understood the wisdom of God. As all his doubts receded, a great sense of peace filled his soul.

Twenty-Six

tNOT MIND

A famous Zen master was sitting on the bank of the river when a scientist from the local town approached him, bowed and asked, "What is the essence of your teaching?"

The master looked at him and did not utter a single word.

The scientist thought to himself, "He is very old and probably already has poor hearing."So he shouted, "You don't seem to hear me! I ask, what is the essence of your message?

The master looked at him and laughed.

"This is strange," the philosopher thought, "At first, he did not answer and now he laughs! But since he did not answer my question, maybe he did not hear anything."

And then the scientist shouted even louder, "I asked what is the essence of your teaching?"

The master calmly replied, "At first, I answered with silence. But you could not understand this, and I had to go easier on you. When you asked the second time, I answered with laughter and joy. But you could not understand even that. Therefore, I have to go down to basics." Then the master scribbled the word 'meditation' on the sand with his finger and concluded, "This is my teaching."

The slightly irritated scientist asked, "Could you clarify your thought?"

Then the master wrote on the sand in larger letters - 'MEDITATION'.

The scientist became even more irritated and said, "Are you joking with me? I ask you to clarify your thought, and you write the same thing, only in larger letters. I'm a famous scientist!"

"Why didn't you tell this right away!" The master exclaimed and scribbled on the sand - 'NOT MIND'.

Twenty-Seven

VERY GREEDY WIFE

A great Zen master named Mokusen lived in a temple in the district of Tanba, Japan. One of his adherents complained of his wife's stinginess. Mokusen visited the adherent's wife and put his clenched fist before her face.

"What do you mean by that?" the surprised woman asked.

"If my fist were always like that, what would you call it?" Mokusen said.

"Deformed," replied the woman.

Then he opened his hand flat, held it in front of her face, and asked, "And if my hand were always like that, what would you call it?"

"Another kind of deformity," said the wife.

"If you understand that much, you are a good wife," said Mokusen and left. After his visit, the wife helped her husband to both save and distribute money.

Twenty-Eight

WHO IS MORE SPIRITUALLY ADVANCED?

One meditation teacher was traveling with his students and one day he heard them argue who among them was more spiritually advanced.

"I've been meditating for fifteen years," said one.

"I have been doing only good deeds since I left my father's house," said another.

"I always follow the Buddha's teachings," said the third.

At noon they stopped under an apple tree's shadow to rest. The branches, weighed down by ripe apples, were almost bent to the ground.

Then the teacher addressed his students, "When a tree bears fruit generously, its branches bend lower and lower. Just so a true sage is humble. When a tree is fruitless, its branches rise arrogantly higher and higher. Just so a fool always considers himself better than his neighbor."

Twenty-Nine

HEAVEN AND HELL

One samurai came to Hakuin, a great Zen master and asked, "Is there really a paradise and a hell?"

"Who are you?" inquired Hakuin.

"I am a warrior," the samurai responded.

"You call yourself a warrior!" exclaimed Hakuin. "What kind of king would have you as his guard? You look like a beggar!"

Hearing these words, the samurai became so enraged that he began to draw his sword, but Hakuin continued, "So you have a sword! Your weapon is probably much too dull to cut off my head."

As the angry warrior brandished his weapon, Hakuin remarked, "Here, open the gates of hell!" At these words, the samurai, perceiving the master's discipline, sheathed his sword and bowed.

"Here, open the gates of paradise," said Hakuin.

Thirty

DOKEN AND SOGEN

A student monk named Doken had spent many years studying without much progress. One day the master sent Doken to a distant place on an errand that would take six months to complete. Doken was very discouraged because this task would hinder his study of Zen meditation.

Doken's friend and fellow monk, Sogen, took pity on him and said, "I will accompany you and help you in whatever way I can so that you can continue to study even while traveling."

So both of them set off on the errand. One evening Sogen said sadly to Doken, "You know, I am willing to help you in every way, but there are five things I can not do for you."

"What are they?" asked Doken.

"When you are hungry or thirsty, you must eat or drink by yourself. My eating will not fill your stomach. When you need to respond to the calls of nature, you must take care of them yourself; I can not be of any use. And then, in traveling, you must carry your own body along this highway," said his Sogen.

With these remarks, Doken's mind was opened. Seeing the change in his friend, Sogen then concluded, "My work is done. You don't need my company any longer," and he left. When Doken finished the errand and returned to the temple, everyone immediately perceived the enlightenment of Doken.

Thirty-One

THE REAL TREASURE

Eno, the sixth patriarch of Zen, received from the fifth patriarch the symbols of authority: the bowl and robe. Because of the jealousy of some of the other monks, Eno left the monastery at night taking the bowl and robe with him. Some monks pursued him, intending to wrest the treasured objects from him. Among them was a tall, powerful monk named Emyo. Eno, being an enlightened master, knew who was following him and waited patiently.

When Emyo appeared, Eno said to him, "These objects simply symbolize the truth. If you want them, take them."

But when Emvo tried to lift the bowl and robe, they were as heavy as mountains. Trembling with shame, he said, "I came for the knowledge, not material treasures. Please teach me."

Eno instructed him, "Do not think of good; do not think of evil. Show me, instead, your true face."

At these words, Emyo became enlightened. With gratitude he said, "You have given me the secret words and meanings. Is there yet a deeper part of the teaching?"

Eno replied, "What I have told you is no secret. When you realize your true self, the secret belongs to you."

Thirty-Two

HAVING A TEMPER

A student came to his Zen master and complained, "Master, I have an uncontrollable temper. How can I cure it?"

"You have something very strange. Let me see what you have," the master responded.

"I can not show it to you at this moment," asked the student.

"When can you show it to me?"

"It arises unexpectedly."

"Then it must not be your own true nature. If it were, you could show it to me at any time. You were not born with it. It is not you," the master concluded.

Thirty-Three

NO MORE QUESTIONS

Upon meeting a Zen master at a social event, a psychiatrist decided to ask him a question that had been on his mind. "Exactly how do you help people?" the doctor inquired.

"I get them where they can't ask any more questions," the master answered.

HARD WORK

A martial arts student went to his teacher and said earnestly, "I am devoted to studying your martial system. How long will it take me to master it?"

The teacher said casually, "Ten years."

Impatiently, the student exclaimed, "This is a long time! I want to master it faster than that. For that, I will work very hard. If I practice ten or more hours a day every day, how long will it take then?"

The teacher thought for a moment and answered, "Twenty years."

Thirty-Five

HEAVY MIND

Hogen, a great Zen teacher, lived alone in a small temple in the country. One day four traveling monks appeared and asked if they might make a fire in his yard to warm themselves.

While they were building the fire, Hogen heard them arguing about subjectivity and objectivity. He joined them and asked, "There is a big stone. Do you consider it to be inside or outside your mind?"

One of the monks responded, "From the Buddhist viewpoint everything is an objectification of mind, so I would say that the stone is inside my mind."

"Your head must feel very heavy," observed Hogen, "if you are carrying around a stone like that in your mind."

Thirty-Six

THE BUDDHA'S NATURE

"The Buddhist scriptures state that everything has a Buddha nature. Do I have a Buddha nature?" One disciple asked his master in the monastery.

"No, you don't have a Buddha nature," the master responded.

"Do trees, rivers, and mountains have a Buddha nature?" The disciple continued asking.

"Yes, trees, rivers and mountains all have a Buddha nature," the master replied.

"Do cats and dogs have a Buddha nature?"

"Yes, cats and dogs, everything in the whole wide world has a Buddha nature!"

"If everything has a Buddha nature, why don't I have a Buddha nature?" Asked a confused disciple.

"Because you are asking!"

Thirty-Seven

LETTING OTHERS DECIDE

"Master, you said that if I understand my true nature, I will become enlightened. But how do I do that?" One disciple asked his Zen master.

"First, you have to take back a right to decide who you are."

"How is that?"

"One person will tell you that you are bad. You will get upset. Another person will tell you that you are good. You will get happy. People can praise you, they can berate you, they can trust you, or they can betray you. While they have a right to decide who you are, you won't find yourself. Take that right back. From me as well."

Thirty-Eight

DEALING WITH A SNOWFALL

One night there was a severe snowstorm in the province where a Zen monastery was located. In the morning, the disciples, waist-deep in the snow, made their way to the meditation hall. Their Zen master asked, "Tell me, what should be done now?"

"We should all meditate on thaw so that the snow melts," the first disciple answered.

"We should wait in our cells and allow the snow to take its natural course," the second disciple responded.

"The one who saw the truth does not care if there is snow or not," the third disciple replied.

The master cast a look around and sighted. "Now listen to what I will say," he said, "Everyone take a shovel and off you go!"

Thirty-Nine

THE POINT OF FASTING

One disciple came to his Zen master after a long solitary practice in the desert and asked, "Master, I felt so much hunger every day during my retreat. When I was living in the monastery, I had never felt this hunger before - I could go for days without food. Why is that?"

"Don't be surprised. There was nobody in the desert to witness your fasting austerity, nobody to support you, nobody to praise you. When you lived in the monastery, the pride and pleasure you received from all of the attention was your food. No wonder you were not hungry!"

Forty

BAD SEEDS

"Why bad inclinations, as opposed to good inclinations, can easily overtake a person?" Asked a disciple his Zen master.

The master replied, "What happens if a good seed is left in the open sun while a bad seed is put into the ground?"

"The good seed left without soil will die, and a bad seed will take root and give bad fruit."

"Just so. Instead of doing good humbly and nourishing the good seeds deep inside the heart, people flaunt them openly, leaving them without any opportunity to grow. Yet, the bad seeds are hidden deep inside where they grow right through a person's heart."

Forty-One

PROPER INTRODUCTION

Keichu, the great Zen teacher of the Meiji era, was the head of a cathedral in Kyoto. One day the governor of Kyoto called upon him for the first time.

His attendant presented the card of the governor, which read: Kitagaki, Governor of Kyoto.

"I have no business with such a fellow," said Keichu to his attendant. "Tell him to get out of here."

The attendant carried the card back with apologies. "That was my error," said the governor, and with a pencil, he scratched out the words Governor of Kyoto. "Ask your teacher again."

"Oh, is that Kitagaki?" exclaimed the teacher when he saw the card. "I want to see that fellow."

Forty-Two

WHAT GOOD IS MEDITATION FOR?

One man asked a famous spiritual teacher skeptically, "What have you gained through meditation?"

The teacher replied, "Nothing at all."

"Then what good is it?"

"This is what I lost through meditation: sickness, anger, depression, insecurity, the burden of old age, the fear of death."

Forty-Three

TRUE AGE

One day Nansen, an elderly Zen master, delayed taking his seat in the dining room. His disciple and chief monk took the master's seat instead of his own.

The master said, "That seat belongs to the oldest monk in this monastery. How old are you?"

"My age goes back to the time of the prehistoric Buddha," responded the chief monk.

"Then," Nansen said, "you are my grandson. Move down."

Forty-Four

ℒIKE A CUP OF TEA

∽ৡৡ∾

A university professor went to visit a famous master Nan-on to inquire about Zen doctrine. While the master quietly served tea, the professor talked about Zen. The master poured the visitor's cup to the brim, and then kept pouring.

The professor watched the overflowing cup until he could no longer restrain himself. "It's overfull! No more will go in!" the professor blurted.

"You are like this cup, full of your own opinions," the master replied. "How can I show you Zen unless you first empty your cup. There is no room for anything else."

Forty-Five

TEACHING ZEN

A young physician named Kusuda wanted to find a true Zen master who wasn't afraid of death. The doctor heard of a great teacher Nan-in and decided to visit him. To determine whether or not the master was afraid to die, Kusuda was secretly carrying a dagger nine and a half inches long.

When Nan-in saw Kusuda, he exclaimed, "Hello, dear friend. How are you? We haven't seen each other for a long time!"

Puzzled Kusuda replied, "But we have never met before."

"That's right," answered Nan-in. "I mistook you for another physician who is receiving instruction here."

With such an introduction, Kusuda lost his chance to test the master, yet he decided to ask if he could receive Zen instruction.

Nan-in said, "Zen is not difficult. If you are a physician, treat your patients with kindness. That is Zen."

The doctor visited Nan-in three times. Each time Nan-in told him the same thing. "A physician should not waste time around here. Go home and take care of your patients."

It was not yet clear to Kusuda how such teaching could remove the fear of death. So on his fourth visit, he asked for more detailed instructions. Nan-in smiled and presented Kusuda with Mu (No-Thing) to work over, the first mind-enlightening problem in the book called The Gateless Gate.

Kusuda pondered this problem of Mu for three and a half years. With such a prolonged practice in concentration, his mind became placid and fears of death dissolved. At last, the doctor could all of his time and focus on treating his patients.

Forty-Six

AMAZING FEATS

One disciple was bragging about his master to the disciple of another master. He claimed that his teacher was capable of all sorts of magical acts, like writing in the air with a brush and having the characters appear on a piece of paper hundreds of feet away. "And what can YOUR master do?" he asked the other disciple.

"My master can also perform amazing feats," the other disciple replied. "When he is tired, he sleeps. When hungry, he eats."

Forty-Seven

NOTHING EXISTS

One brash student of Zen visited a famous master Dokuon.

Desiring to show his attainment and impress the teacher, he said, "The mind, Buddha, and sentient beings, after all, do not exist. The true nature of phenomena is emptiness. There is no master; there is no student. There is no giving; there is no receiving. What we think we see and feel is not real. None of these seeming things really exists."

Dokuon, who was smoking quietly, said nothing. Suddenly he picked up his staff and whacked the student. The young man jumped up in anger.

"If nothing exists," inquired Dokuon, "where did your anger come from?"

Forty-Eight

WHAT'S THE WAY?

One student asked his master, "What is the Way?"

The master replied, "Everyday life is the Way."

"Can it be studied?" the student wondered.

"If you try to study, you will be far away from it."

"If I do not study, how can I know it is the Way?"

"The Way does not belong to the perception world; neither does it belong to the non-perception world. Cognition is a delusion, and non-cognition is senseless. If you want to reach the true Way beyond doubt, place yourself in the same freedom as the sky. You name it neither good nor not-good," the master said.

Forty-Nine

EIGHTY-THREE PROBLEMS

One farmer came to the monastery to seek advice from a famous Zen teacher.

"I like farming," the farmer started, "but sometimes it doesn't rain enough, and my crops fail. Last year we nearly starved. And sometimes it rains too much, so my yields vanish."

The master patiently listened to the man.

"I'm married, too," said the man, "but sometimes my wife nags me too much and I get tired of her."

The master listened quietly.

"I have kids," said the man. "but sometimes they don't show me enough respect."

The man went on like this, laying out all his difficulties and worries. Finally, he wound down and waited for the master to say the words that would put everything right for him.

Instead, the master said, "I can't help you."

"What do you mean?" said the man, astonished.

"Everybody experiences problems," said the Master. "In fact, we've all got eighty-three problems, each one of us. Once you fix one, another problem will appear right in its place. And there's nothing you, I, or anyone else can do about it."

The man became furious and shouted, "I thought you were a great teacher! What is the point of your teaching, then?"

The master said, "My teaching will help you with the eighty-fourth problem."

"The eighty-fourth problem?" said the man. "What's the eighty-fourth problem?"

Replied the master, "You want not to have any problems."

Fifty

THE NEWSPAPERS

One morning a newspaper carrier was pushing his cart along a mountain road. Two Zen monks were walking toward him. One of them was a master, and the other was his student. The student said, "Master, the teaching says that the world is a dream of Buddha; and once you become a Buddha, the world will be your dream. Please explain to me how could there be several awakened ones in the same world?"

Suddenly a gust of wind swept the card, and thousands of newspapers flew up into the air.

"Look," said the master, "there are so many newspapers, but the text in all of them is the same."

Upon hearing this, the student became enlightened.

Fifty-One

SPARING THE KNOWLEDGE

A well-known Zen monk Gasan instructed his students one day, "Those who speak against killing and who desire to spare the lives of all conscious beings are right. It is good to protect even animals and insects. But what about those persons who kill time? What about those who are destroying wealth? We should not overlook them. Furthermore, what of the one who preaches without enlightenment? He is killing Buddhism."

Fifty-Two

WHAT IS MOVING?

Two monks were arguing about a flag flapping in the wind. The first monk said, "The flag is moving."

The second monk contended, "No, the wind is moving."

A Zen master happened to be passing by and, hearing this debate, concluded, "Not the wind, not the flag - the Mind is moving."

Fifty-Three

WAS THERE A SPIDER?

While meditating in his room, one Zen student believed he saw a spider descending in front of him. Each day the menacing creature returned, growing larger and larger each time. So frightened was the student that he went to his master to report this. He said he planned to place a knife in his lap during meditation, so that when the spider appeared, he would kill it. The master advised him against this plan and suggested bringing a piece of chalk to meditation so that when the spider appeared again, the student would mark an "X" on its belly.

With this, the student returned to his meditation room. When the spider again appeared, he resisted the urge to attack it and instead did just what the master suggested. When he later reported back to the master, the teacher told him to lift his shirt and look at his own belly. There was the "X."

Fifty-Four

ZEN DIALOGUE

Two Zen temples located nearby each had a child protégé. One child, going to obtain vegetables each morning, would meet the other on the way.

"Where are you going?" asked the one.

"I am going wherever my feet go," the other responded.

This reply puzzled the first child who went to his teacher for help. "Tomorrow morning," the teacher told him, "when you meet that little fellow, ask him the same question. He will give you the same answer, and then you ask him, 'Suppose you have no feet, then where are you going?' That will fix him."

The children met the following morning again.

"Where are you going?" asked the first child.

"I am going wherever the wind blows," answered the other.

This again puzzled the youngster, who took his defeat to his teacher. "Ask him where he is going if there is no wind," suggested the teacher.

The next day the children met a third time.

"Where are you going?" asked the first child.

"I am going to the market to buy vegetables," the other child responded.

II

THE ART OF ZEN LIVING

"I came from brilliancy. And return to brilliancy. What is this?"

- the last poem of Hoshin, a great Zen master

Fifty-Five

THE EXACT SPOT

One master of tea ceremony wished to hang a flower basket on a column. He asked a carpenter to help him, directing the man to place it slightly higher or lower, to the right or left, until he had found exactly the right spot.

To test the master, the carpenter marked the spot and then pretended he had forgotten.
"Is this the place? Or is this the place, perhaps?" the carpenter kept asking, pointing to various places on the column.

But so accurate was the tea-master's sense of proportion that it was not until the carpenter reached the identical spot again that its location was approved.

Fifty-Six

RIGHT AND WRONG

When Zen master Bankei held his seclusion-weeks of meditation, pupils from many parts of Japan came to attend. During one of these gatherings a pupil was caught stealing. The matter was reported to Bankei requesting the culprit to be expelled. Bankei ignored the case.

Later the pupil was caught in a similar act, and again Bankei disregarded the matter. This angered the other pupils, who drew up a petition asking for the dismissal of the thief, stating that otherwise they would leave immediately.

When Bankei had read the petition, he called everyone before him and said, "You are wise brothers. You know what is right and what is not right. You may go somewhere else to study if you wish, but this poor brother does not even know right from wrong. Who will teach him if I do not? I will keep him here even if all the rest of you leave."

A torrent of tears cleansed the face of the brother who had stolen. All desire to steal had vanished.

Fifty-Seven

SOUR MISO

The cook monk at Bankei's monastery decided that he would take good care of his old teacher's health and give him only fresh miso, a paste of soybeans mixed with wheat and yeast that often ferments. Bankei, noticing that he was being served better miso than his pupils, asked, "Who is the cook today?"

The cook monk was sent before him. From him Bankei learned that according to his age and position the master should eat only fresh miso. So Bankei said to the cook, "Then you think I shouldn't eat at all." With this he entered his room and locked the door.

Sitting outside the door, the cook monk asked for his master's pardon. Bankei would not answer. For seven days the monk sat outside and Bankei within.

Finally, in desperation, an adherent called loudly to Bankei, "You may be all right, old teacher, but this young disciple here has to eat. He cannot go without food forever!"

At that, Bankei opened the door. He smiled and said, "I insist on eating the same food as the least of my followers. When you become the teacher, I do not want you to forget this."

Fifty-Eight

EVERYTHING IS BEST

⁓

When a future Zen master Banza was a young monk, he walked through a market and overheard a conversation between a butcher and his customer.

"Give me the best piece of meat you have," said the customer.

"Everything in my shop is the best," replied the butcher. "You cannot find here any piece that is not the best."

At these words, Banzan became enlightened.

Fifty-Nine

SERVING HUMANITY

Once when a division of the royal army was engaged in a mock combat, some of the officers found it necessary to make their headquarters in a temple of a great Zen master named Gasan.

When the officers arrived, the master ordered to serve them the same simple food as the monks eat. Being used to receiving deferential treatment, the officers were not happy with such a service rendered at the temple.

One man came to Gasan and said, "Who do you think we are? We are soldiers serving the people of our country. Why don't you treat us accordingly?"

Gasan replied sternly, "Who do you think we are? We are soldiers of humanity, serving all sentient beings."

Sixty

SLEEPING IN THE DAYTIME

The master Soyen passed from this world when he was sixty-one years of age. Fulfilling his life's work, the master never wasted a minute and managed to leave a great teaching. While his students used to sleep in the daytime during midsummer, Soyen overlooked this but never slept himself.

When he was twelve years old, he was a student of another great teacher. One summer day, the air was so sultry that little Soyen stretched his legs and went to sleep while his teacher was away. Three hours passed when, suddenly waking, he heard his master entered. It was too late - there he laid, sprawled across the doorway.

"I beg your pardon, I beg your pardon," his teacher whispered, stepping carefully over Soyen's body as if it were that of some distinguished guest. After this, Soyen never slept again in the afternoon.

Sixty-One

THE THIEF WHO BECAME A DISCIPLE

One evening as master Shichiri was reciting sutras, a thief with a sharp sword entered, demanding either money or his life.

Shichiri told him, "Do not disturb me. You can find the money in that drawer." Then he resumed his recitation.

A little while afterwards he stopped and called, "Don't take it all. I need some to pay taxes with tomorrow."

The intruder gathered up most of the money and started to leave. "Thank a person when you receive a gift," Shichiri added. The man thanked him and made off.

A few days after, the fellow was caught and confessed, among others, the offence against Shichiri. When Shichiri was called as a witness, he said, "This man is no thief, at least as far as I am concerned. I gave him money, and he thanked me for it."

After the thief had finished his prison term, he went to Shichiri and became his disciple.

Sixty-Two

THE MAP

Once a famous Zen master defiantly burned a sacred Buddhist scripture. When he was doing this, the students asked him, "Master, what have you done? You have always taught us from these scriptures, commented on them and meditated on them. Why are you burning them now?"

"Because I came home," the master replied, "I no longer need the map."

Sixty-Three

NO WATER, NO MOON

Chiyono, a nun, studied for many years under Zen master Bukko at the temple in Kamakura. Still, she could not attain the fruits of meditation. One moonlight night, she was carrying water carefully in an old wooden pail girded by bamboo. The bamboo broke, and the bottom fell out of the pail. At that moment, she was set free.

Chiyono said, "No more water in the pail, no more moon in the water."

Sixty-Four

NATURE'S BEAUTY

One monk was in charge of the garden within a famous Zen temple. Next to the temple was another, smaller temple where a very old Zen master lived. One day, before a certain celebration, the monk took extra care in tending to the garden. He pulled the weeds, trimmed the shrubs, combed the moss, and spent a long time meticulously raking up and carefully arranging all the dry autumn leaves. As he worked, the old master watched him with interest from across the wall that separated the temples.

When finished with his gardening work, the monk stood back and admired the result. "Master, look here. Isn't it beautiful?" the monk called out to the old master.

"Yes, but something is missing," replied the old man. "Help me over this wall, and I'll put it right for you."

After a slight hesitation, the monk lifted the old fellow over and set him down. Slowly, the master walked to the tree near the garden's center, grabbed it by the trunk, and shook it. Leaves showered down all over the garden. "There," said the old man, "you can put me back now."

Sixty-Five

PUBLISHING THE SUTRAS

Tetsugen, a devotee of Zen in Japan, decided to publish the sutras, which at that time were available only in Chinese. The books were to be printed with wood blocks in an edition of seven thousand copies, a tremendous undertaking.

Tetsugen began by traveling and collecting donations for this purpose. A few sympathizers would give him a hundred pieces of gold, but most of the time he received only small coins. He thanked each donor with equal gratitude. After ten years Tetsugen had enough money to begin his task.

It happened that at that time the Uji River overflowed. Famine followed. Tetsugen took the funds he had collected for the books and spent them to save others from starvation. Then he began his work of collecting again.

Several years afterwards, an epidemic spread over the country. Tetsugen again gave away what he had collected to help his people.

For a third time, he started his work, and after twenty years his wish was fulfilled. The printing blocks which produced the first edition of sutras can be seen today in the Obaku monastery in Kyoto.

Now it is often said that Tetsugen made three sets of sutras and that the first two invisible sets surpass even the last.

Sixty-Six

THE GIFT

Ryokan, a Zen master, lived the simplest kind of life in a little hut at the foot of a mountain. One evening a thief visited the hut only to discover there was nothing in it to steal.

Ryokan returned and caught him. "You may have come a long way to visit me," he told the prowler, "and you should not return empty-handed. Please take my clothes as a gift."

The thief was bewildered. He took the clothes and slunk away.

The master sat naked, watching the moon. "Poor fellow, " he mused, "I wish I could give him this beautiful moon."

Sixty-Seven

THE HAPPIEST MAN

A great master named Hotei lived in the Tang dynasty. He had no desire to call himself a Zen master or to gather many disciples around him. Instead, he walked the streets with a big sack into which he would put gifts of candy, fruit, or doughnuts. These he would give to children who gathered around him in play. He established a kindergarten on the streets.

Whenever he met a Zen devotee, he would extend his hand and say, "Give me one penny."

Once as he was about to play-work, another Zen master happened to walk along and inquired, "What is the significance of Zen?"

Hotei immediately plopped his sack down on the ground in a silent answer.

"Then," asked the other, "what is the actualization of Zen?"

At once Hotei swung the sack over his shoulder and continued on his way.

Sixty-Eight

CHILDREN OF HIS MAJESTY

Yamaoka was a tutor of the emperor. He was also a master of fencing and a profound student of Zen.

His home was the abode of vagabonds. He has but one suit of clothes, for they kept him always poor.

Observing how worn his garments were, the emperor gave Yamaoka some money to buy new ones. The next time Yamaoka appeared, he wore the same old outfit.

"What became of the new clothes, Yamaoka?" asked the emperor.

"I provided clothes for the children of Your Majesty," explained Yamaoka.

Sixty-Nine

MIDNIGHT EXCURSION

Many students were studying meditation under the Zen master Sengai. One of them used to arise at night, climb over the temple wall, and go to town on a pleasure jaunt.

Sengai, inspecting the dormitory quarters, found this student missing one night and also discovered the high stool he had used to scale the wall. Sengai removed the stool and stood there in its place.

When the wanderer returned, not knowing that Sengai was the stool, he put his feet on the master's head and jumped down into the grounds. Discovering what he had done, he was aghast.

Sengai said, "It is very chilly in the early morning. Do be careful not to catch a cold yourself."

The student never went out at night again.

Seventy

IS THAT SO?

⎯⎯ ᘐᘗᗢᗢᘖ ⎯⎯

Zen master Hakuin was greatly respected and had many disciples. At one time in his life, he lived in a village hermitage, close to a food shop run by a couple and their beautiful young daughter. One day the parents discovered that their daughter was pregnant. Angry and distraught, they demanded to know the name of the father. At first, the girl would not confess but after much harassment, she named Hakuin. The furious parents confronted Hakuin, berating him in front of all of his students. He simply replied, "Is that so?"

When the baby was born, the family gave it to Hakuin. By this time, he had lost his reputation and his disciples. But Hakuin was not disturbed. He took delight in caring for the infant child; he was able to obtain milk and other essentials from the villagers. A year later, the child's young mother was troubled by great remorse. She confessed the truth to her parents – the real father was not Hakuin but rather a young man who worked at the local fish market. The mortified parents went to Hakuin, apologizing, asking his forgiveness for the wrong they did him. They asked Hakuin to return the baby. Although he loved the child as his own, Hakuin was willing to give him up without complaint. All he said was, "Is that so?"

SAVING A SNAKE

One Zen monk saw that a snake got caught in a fire and decided to save it. He reached into the fire, grabbed the reptile and dragged it out. As he was doing it, the snake bit the monk several times, causing him great pain. Yet, the monk didn't let go until the snake was saved.

Seeing this, one of the monk's students exclaimed, "The snake bit you! Why did you still proceed to save it?"

"The nature of a snake is to bite, but it does not change my nature - to help," the monk replied.

Seventy-Two

A TRUE MASTERPIECE

At Obaku temple in Kyoto one can see the words "The First Principle" carved over the gate. The letters are unusually large, and those who appreciate calligraphy always admire them as a masterpiece. They were drawn by master Kosen two hundred years ago.

When the master drew them, he did so on paper, from which workers made the larger carving in wood. As Kosen sketched the letters, one of his especially perceptive students was watching him. When the master finished his first effort, he asked for the student's opinion.

"That is not good," the student told Kosen.

"How is that one?"

"Poor. Worse than before," pronounced the student.

Kosen patiently wrote one sheet after another until eighty-four First Principles had been accumulated, still without the approval of the student.

Then, when the young man stepped outside for a few moments, Kosen thought, "Now is my chance to escape his keen eye," and hurriedly wrote with a mind free from distraction.

"This is a masterpiece!" exclaimed the student upon return.

Seventy-Three

SURPRISING THE MASTER

The students in the monastery were in total awe of the elder monk, not because he was strict, but because nothing ever seemed to upset or ruffle him. They found him a bit unearthly, so they decided to put him to the test. A bunch of them very quietly hid in a dark corner of one of the hallways and waited for the monk to walk by. Within moments, the old man appeared carrying a cup of hot tea. Just as he passed by, the students all rushed out at him screaming as loud as they could. But the old monk showed no reaction whatsoever. He peacefully made his way to a small table at the end of the hall, gently placed the cup down, and then, leaning against the wall, cried out with shock, "Ohhhhh!"

Seventy-Four

TWO MONKS AND A WOMAN

Two celibate monks were traveling from one monastery to another. After a long walk, they came to a river they had to cross. The river was flooded, and there was no way that they would get across without getting wet. One lady was also at the banks of that river, wanting to cross; she was weeping because she was afraid to cross on her own.

The monks decided to cross the river by walking through the relatively shallow part of the river. Since the lady also needed to get to the other bank, the older monk, without much ado, carried her on his shoulders, and soon they reached the other bank, where he set her down. The lady went her way, and the two monks continued their walk in silence. The younger monk was very upset, finding the other monk's act disturbing.

After a few hours, the younger monk couldn't stand the thought of what had happened, which kept filling his mind, and so he began to berate the other monk saying, "We are not allowed to look at women, but you carried that woman!"

"Which woman?" replied the older monk.

"The woman you carried on your shoulders across the river!"

The other monk paused and with a smile on his lips said, "I put her down when I crossed the river. Why are you still carrying her?"

Seventy-Five

NO WORK, NO FOOD

Hyakujo, the Chinese Zen master, used to labor with his students even at the age of eighty, trimming the gardens, cleaning the grounds, and pruning the trees.

The students felt sorry to see the old master working so hard, but they knew he would not listen to their advice to stop, so they hid away his tools.

That day the master did not eat. The next day he did not eat, nor the next. "He may be angry because we have hidden his tools," the students surmised. "We had better put them back."

The day they did, the master worked and ate the same as before. In the evening, he instructed them, "No work, no food."

SPECIAL GUIDELINES

Zengetsu, a Chinese master of the Tang dynasty, wrote the following advice for his students:

Living in the world yet not forming attachments to the dust of the world is the way of a true Zen student.

When witnessing the good action of another, encourage yourself to follow his example. Hearing of the mistaken action of another, advise yourself not to emulate it.

Even though alone in a dark room, be as if you were facing a noble guest. Express your feelings, but become no more expressive than your true nature.

Poverty is your treasure. Never exchange it for an easy life.

A person may appear a fool and yet not be one. He may only be guarding his wisdom carefully.

Virtues are the fruit of self-discipline and do not drop from heaven of themselves as does rain or snow.

Modesty is the foundation of all virtues. Let your neighbors discover you before you make yourself known to them.

A noble heart never forces itself forward. Its words are as rare gems, seldom displayed and of great value.

To a sincere student, every day is a fortunate day. Time passes, but he never lags behind. Neither glory nor shame can move him.

Censure yourself, never another. Do not discuss right and wrong.

Some things, though right, were considered wrong for generations. Since the value of righteousness may be recognized after centuries, there is no need to crave an immediate appreciation.

Live with cause and leave results to the great law of the universe. Pass each day in peaceful contemplation.

III

THE ART OF ZEN DYING

"Sixty-six times have these eyes beheld the changing scene of autumn. I have said enough about moonlight. Ask no more. Only listen to the voice of pines and cedars when no wind stirs."

- Ryonen, Zen Buddhist nun

Seventy-Seven

THE EMPEROR'S QUESTIONS

Once the emperor Goyozei, who was studying Zen at the time, asked his master named Gudo, "In Zen doctrine this very mind is Buddha. Is this correct?"

The master responded, "If I say yes, you will think that you understand without understanding. If I say no, I would contradict a fact you may understand quite well."

Then the emperor asked, "Where does the enlightened man go when he dies?"

Gudo answered, "I know not."

"Why don't you know?"asked the emperor.

"Because I have not died yet," replied the master.

After that, the emperor stopped inquiring about things his mind could not grasp.

Seventy-Eight

THE RIGHT SUCCESSOR

The old Zen master's health was fading. Knowing his death was near, he announced to all the monks that he soon would be passing down his robe and rice bowl to appoint the next master of the monastery. His choice, he said, would be based on a contest. Anyone seeking the appointment was required to demonstrate his spiritual wisdom by submitting a poem.

The head monk, the most obvious successor, presented a poem that was well composed and insightful. All the monks anticipated his selection as their new leader. However, the next morning another poem appeared on the wall in the hallway, apparently written during the dark hours of the night. It stunned everyone with its elegance and profundity but no one knew who the author was. Determined to find this person, the old master began questioning all the monks. To his surprise, the investigation led to the rather quiet kitchen worker who pounded rice for the meals. Upon hearing the news, the jealous head monk and his comrades plotted to kill their rival.

In secret, the old master passed down his robe and bowl to the rice pounder, who quickly fled from the monastery, later to become a widely renowned Zen teacher.

Seventy-Nine

THE SECRET TO PROSPERITY

A rich man asked one Zen master to write something down that could encourage the prosperity of his family for years to come, something that the family could cherish for generations. On a large piece of paper the master wrote, "Father dies, son dies, grandson dies."

The rich man became angry when he saw the master's work and said, "I asked you to write something down that could bring happiness and prosperity to my family. Why did you give me this?"

"If your son should die before you," the master answered, "this would bring unbearable grief to your family. If your grandson should die before your son, this also would bring great sorrow. If your family, generation after generation, disappears in the order I have described, it will be the natural course of life. This is true happiness and prosperity."

Eighty

THE DREAM

~⚬⚬⚬~

The great master Chuang Tzu once dreamt that he was a butterfly fluttering here and there. In this dream he had no awareness of his individuality as a person - he was only a butterfly. Suddenly, he awoke and found himself laying there, a person once again. But then he thought to himself, "Was I before a man who dreamt about being a butterfly, or am I now a butterfly who dreams about being a man?"

Eighty-One

THE TUNNEL

Zenkai, the son of a samurai, journeyed to Edo and there became the retainer of a high official. He fell in love with the official's wife and was discovered. In self-defence, he slew the official. Then he ran away with the wife. Both of them later became thieves. But the woman was so greedy that Zenkai grew disgusted. Finally, leaving her, he journeyed far away to the province of Buzen, where he became a wandering mendicant.

To atone for his past, Zenkai resolved to accomplish some good deed in his lifetime. Knowing of a dangerous road over a cliff that had caused death and injury to many persons, he resolved to cut a tunnel through the mountain there.

Begging food in the daytime, Zenkai worked at night digging his tunnel. When thirty years had gone by, the tunnel was 2,280 feet long, 20 feet high, and 30 feet wide.

Two years before the work was completed, the son of the official he had slain, who was a skillful swordsman, found Zenkai out and came to kill him in revenge.

"I will give you my life willingly," said Zenkai. "Only let me finish this work. On the day it is completed, then you may kill me."

So the son awaited the day. Several months passed and Zenkai kept digging. The son grew tired of doing nothing and began to help with the digging. After he had helped for more than a year, he came to admire Zenkai's strong will and character.

At last the tunnel was completed and the people could use it and travel safely.

"Now cut off my head," said Zenkai. "My work is done."

"How can I cut off my own teacher's head?" asked the younger man with tears in his eyes.

Eighty-Two

WITHOUT FEAR

During the civil wars in feudal Japan, an invading army would quickly sweep into a town and take control. In one particular village, everyone fled just before the army arrived - everyone except the Zen master. Curious about this old fellow, the general went to the temple to see for himself what kind of man this master was. When he wasn't treated with the deference and submissiveness to which he was accustomed, the general burst into anger.

"You fool, don't you realize you are standing before a man who could run you through without blinking an eye!" the general shouted as he reached for his sword. But despite the threat, the master seemed unmoved.

"And do you realize that you are standing before a man who can be run through without blinking an eye?" the master replied calmly.

Eighty-Three

THE PATH REVEALED

Just before one spiritual teacher passed away the great Zen master named Ikkyu paid him a visit.

"Shall I lead you on?" Ikkyu asked.

The teacher answered, "What can you do for me? I came here alone and I will go alone."

"If you think you really come and go, you are immersed in a delusion. Let me show you the path on which there is no coming and going," said Ikkyu.

And by saying this Ikkyu had revealed the path so clearly that the teacher smiled and passed away in peace.

Eighty-Four

TIME TO DIE

A Zen master Ikkyu was very clever even as a boy. His teacher, an old monk, had a rare antique teacup. Ikkyu happened to break this cup and was greatly perplexed. Hearing the footsteps of his teacher, he held the pieces of the cup behind him. When the master appeared, Ikkyu asked, "Why do people have to die?"

"This is a natural order," explained the old monk. "Everything has to die and has just so long to live."

Ikkyu, producing the shattered cup, added, "I think it was time for your cup to die."

IV

ZEN PARABLES

"For fifty-six years I lived as best I could,
Making my way in this world.
Now the rain has ended, the clouds are clearing,
The blue sky has a full moon."

- the last poem of Shoan, a great master of Soto Zen

MAY BE

A long time ago lived an old farmer who had worked his crops for many years. One day his only horse ran away. His friends and neighbors came by to console him, saying what a bad luck it was to lose such a great animal. But the old man didn't seem particularly bothered and simply replied, "May be."

Sure enough, a few days later, the horse returned and brought three other wild horses with it. "Congratulations, how wonderful!" said the neighbors. "May be," the old farmer responded.

Sometime later, when the old man's son tried to ride one of the untamed horses, he was thrown off and broke his leg. When it became clear that the son would have a bad limp for the rest of his life, the neighbors again came to offer the old man their sympathy. Unmoved, the old man said, "May be."

The next day, military officials came to the village to draft young men into the army. As the old man's son had a broken leg, the officials passed him by. Seeing how things turned out, the neighbours congratulated the farmer. "May be," once again responded the old man.

Eighty-Six

TRANSIENT NATURE

One hermit came to the front door of the King's palace. None of the guards tried to stop him as he entered and made his way to where the King himself was sitting on his throne.

"What do you want?" asked the King.

"I would like a place to sleep in this inn," replied the hermit.

"But this is not an inn," said the King, "It is my palace."

"May I ask who owned this palace before you?"

"My father. He is dead."

"And who owned it before him?"

"My grandfather. He too is dead."

"So if this is a place where people live for a short time and then move on, how is it NOT an inn?"

Eighty-Seven

REACHING ENLIGHTENMENT

One master was walking up to the mountain and came across three people: a man sitting and meditating under the tree shadow, a man sitting and meditating in the sun, and a man dancing away. All three of them were on their path to enlightenment.

When the master passed the first man, the latter asked, "When will I get enlightened?"

The master answered that it would take at least a thousand years for him to get enlightened. The man continued meditating under the tree.

The master then passed the second man who was sitting in the sun. Parts of his skin were severely burnt, but the man continued meditating and stopped only to ask the same question, "How long would it take for me to get enlightened?"

The master told him that it would take at least another thousand years for him to get enlightened. On hearing this, the man thought, 'I have to suffer so much to get enlightened,' and continued meditating in the sun.

As the master passed the third person who was dancing, he heard the same question. Once again the master said, "It will take you another thousand years to get enlightened."

The man had a laugh and continued dancing. At that instance, he got enlightened.

Eighty-Eight

THE VALUE OF SILENCE

Four monks decided to meditate silently without speaking for two weeks. By nightfall on the first day, the candle began to flicker and then went out.

The first monk said, "Oh, no! The candle is out."

The second monk said, "Aren't we not supposed to talk?"

The third monk said, "Why must you two break the silence?"

The fourth monk laughed and said, "Ha! I'm the only one who didn't speak."

Eighty-Nine

IN THE HANDS OF DESTINY

A great general decided to attack the enemy, although he had only one-tenth the number of men the opposition commanded. He knew that he would win, but his soldiers were in doubt.

On the way, he stopped at a temple and told his men, "After I visit the shrine, I will toss a coin. If heads comes, we will win; if tails, we will lose. Destiny holds us in her hand."

The general entered the shrine and offered a silent prayer. He came forth and tossed a coin. Heads appeared. His soldiers were so eager to fight that they won their battle easily.

"No one can change the hand of destiny," his attendant told him after the battle.

"Indeed not," said the general, showing a coin which had been doubled, with heads facing either way.

Ninety

TRUE GIVING

One day, when the Buddhist monks were out collecting food donations for their temple, one monk entered the yard of a house that looked so poor he felt guilty about asking them for anything. He turned around and was leaving when the owner called out to him. His family had very little, but they wanted to make an offering. They added a bit of rice to the water and boiled it down until it thickened a bit. Using their best bowl and a serving table, the family offered a bowl of this rice water to the monk, who humbly accepted it.

As the monk drank the rice water, he was moved to tears by their sincerity and wanted to do something to help them. He had nothing of his own to give, but he could find them some firewood. So, later in the day, he took up an empty pack and headed into the mountains. He collected all the wood he could carry and was on his way to their house when he met his teacher, the head monk.

The teacher asked him what he was doing, and the monk explained the whole story to him. As soon as the monk finished, his teacher swung his staff around and started beating the monk's legs mercilessly, exclaiming, "What do you think you're doing? For years now you've been studying this vast and profound fundamental mind! You should be helping them through formless giving! Once they've burnt up that wood, your help is gone!"

Stunned, the monk jumped up, suddenly understanding the formless giving. When his pain and shock were gone, the monk felt so light. Taking all of his gratitude and best wishes for the family, he silently entrusted them to his foundation. Before too long, the family that had given him the rice water began to flourish.

Ninety-One

THE WORDS SHOULD BE KIND

Once, long ago, a poor farmer was given an ox calf in repayment for a debt. The farmer, grateful for the present, called the calf Great Joy and cared for him well.

As he grew, Great Joy became a formidable bull, powerful in appearance and in strength. He helped in the field, pulling the plow, rooting out tree stumps and digging up rocks from the ground. It was not needed to hit his sides or his back to get the job done - it was enough to say 'Pull!' and Great Joy knew immediately what he had to do.

Once the farmer made a bet with a local merchant that Great Joy would pull a hundred loaded carts at once for a thousand silver coins. The farmer put a harness on the ox and tied one cart after another - a hundred carts in total loaded to the brim. By the time he was finished, a big crowd had gathered around the powerful animal. Not wanting to embarrass himself in front of the townsfolk, the farmer decided to hit the ox with a whip.

But Great Joy did not pull; he did not even twitch a muscle to scare a fly off his hide. The farmer then started to rebuke and scream at the poor animal. Not being used to such rude treatment, the ox didn't move a bit. The wager was lost.

The farmer didn't sleep the whole night and in the morning decided to place another bet. This time, when Great Joy was harnessed to a hundred loaded carts, the farmer gently tapped the mighty neck and whispered great words of affection into the ox's ear. And Great Joy sank his hooves into the ground, tensed all the muscles of his body and pressed forward. The boards of all one hundred carts began to groan. A thick silence fell over everyone who saw this. Now the bet was won by the farmer, who made a promise to never be rude and unkind to people and animals alike.

Ninety-Two

MEETING A HOLY MAN

Rumours spread that the wise Holy Man lived in a small house atop the mountain. A young man from the village decided to climb the mountain to visit him. When after a long and difficult journey, he arrived at the house on top of the mountain, all he saw was an old servant standing at the door.

"I would like to see the wise Holy Man," the young man said to the servant. With a smile, the servant led him inside the house. As they walked through the house, the young man looked eagerly around the house, expecting his encounter with the Holy Man. But before he knew it, he had been led to the back door and escorted outside. He stopped and turned to the servant, "But I want to see the Holy Man!"

"You already have," said the old man. "See everyone you may meet in life, no matter how plain and insignificant they appear, as a wise Holy Man."

Ninety-Three

FACING THE DEMONS

An old hermit lived in isolation in a cave on the side of a mountain. One day when he returned after a long walk, he found that seven demons had moved into his cave. The hermit tried everything to make them leave: he prayed to his teachers, cried out in a loud voice, meditated, demanded the demons to go, but alas, to no avail. The demons only grew bigger and stronger.

Realizing that the demons were simply visible projections of his inner mind, the hermit then decided to try something different. He smiled and said to the demons, "Welcome to my home, all that I have is yours," whereupon all demons but one disappeared. And the last demon, the most persistent one, continued to rampage through his house.

At a loss for what to do, the hermit finally said, "You may have not only my home but my life as well," and he walked up to the demon and put his head into the demon's mouth. In that moment of full surrender, the final demon had too disappeared.

Ninety-Four

THE GIFT OF INSULTS

A long time ago lived a great warrior. Even when he got very old, he still could defeat any challenger. As his reputation extended far and wide throughout the land, many followers gathered to study under him.

One day a young warrior arrived at the village who wanted to become the first man to defeat the great master. Along with his strength, he had an uncanny ability to spot and exploit any weakness in an opponent. He would wait for his opponent to make the first move, thus revealing a weakness, and then strike with merciless force and lightning speed. No one had ever lasted with him in a match beyond the first move.

Much against the advice of his concerned students, the old master gladly accepted the young warrior's challenge. As the two squared off for battle, the young warrior began to hurl insults at the old master. He threw dirt and spit in his face. He verbally assaulted him with every curse and insult known to mankind for hours. But the old warrior merely stood there motionless and calm. Finally, the young warrior exhausted himself. Knowing he was defeated, he left feeling shamed.

Somewhat disappointed that he did not fight the insolent youth, the students gathered around the old master and questioned him. "How could you endure such an indignity? How did you drive him away?"

"If someone comes to give you a gift and you do not receive it," the master replied, "to whom does the gift belong?"

Ninety-Five

STONE CUTTER

There was once a stone cutter who was dissatisfied with himself and his position in life. One day he passed a wealthy merchant's house. Through the open gateway, he saw many fine possessions and important visitors. "How powerful that merchant must be!" thought the stone cutter. He became very envious and wished that he could be like the merchant.

To his great surprise, he suddenly became the merchant, enjoying more luxuries and power than he had ever imagined, but envied and detested by those less wealthy than himself. Soon a high official passed by, carried in a sedan chair, accompanied by attendants and escorted by soldiers beating gongs. Everyone, no matter how wealthy, had to bow low before the procession. "How powerful that official is!" he thought. "I wish that I could be a high official!"

Then he became the high official, carried everywhere in his embroidered sedan chair, feared and hated by people all around. It was a hot summer day, so the official felt very uncomfortable in the sticky sedan chair. He looked up at the sun. It shone proudly in the sky, unaffected by his presence. "How powerful the sun is!" he thought. "I wish that I could be the sun!"

Then he became the sun, shining fiercely down on everyone, scorching the fields, cursed by the farmers and labourers. But a huge black cloud moved between him and the earth so that his light could no longer shine on everything below. "How powerful that storm cloud is!" he thought. "I wish that I could be a cloud!"

Then he became the cloud, flooding the fields and villages, shouted at by everyone. But soon he found that he was being pushed away by some great force and realized that it was the wind. "How powerful it is!" he thought. "I wish that I could be the wind!"

Then he became the wind, blowing tiles off the roofs of houses, uprooting trees, feared and hated by all below him. But after a while, he ran up against something that would not move, no matter how forcefully he blew against it - a huge towering rock. "How powerful that rock is!" he thought. "I wish that I could be a rock!"

Then he became the rock, more powerful than anything else on earth. But as he stood there, he heard a hammer pounding a chisel into the hard surface and felt himself being changed. "What could be more powerful than I, the rock?" he thought.

He looked down and saw the figure of a stone cutter far below him.

Ninety-Six

WINNING A DEBATE

Provided he makes and wins an argument about Buddhism with those who live there, any wandering monk can remain in a Zen temple. If he is defeated, he has to move on. In a temple in the northern part of Japan two brother monks were dwelling together. The elder one was learned, but the younger one was stupid and had but one eye.

A wandering monk came and asked for lodging, properly challenging them to a debate about the sublime teaching. The elder brother, tired that day from much studying, told the younger one to take his place. "Go and request the dialogue in silence," he cautioned.

So the young monk and the stranger went to the shrine and sat down.

Shortly afterwards, the traveler rose and went to the elder brother and said, "Your young brother is a wonderful fellow. He defeated me."

"Relate the dialogue to me," inquired the elder brother.

"First, I held up one finger, representing Buddha, the enlightened one. So he held up two fingers, signifying Buddha and his teaching. I held up three fingers, representing Buddha, his teaching, and his followers living a harmonious life. Then he shook his clenched fist in my face, indicating that all three come from one realization. Thus he won, and so I have no right to remain here," explained the traveler, bowed and left.

"Where is that fellow?" asked the younger one, running into his elder brother. "I'm going to beat him up."

"Tell me the subject of the debate," asked the elder one.

"Why, the minute he saw me, he held up one finger, insulting me by insinuating that I have only one eye. Since he was a stranger, I thought I would be polite to him, so I held up two fingers, congratulating him that he has two eyes. Then the impolite wretch held up three fingers, suggesting that we only have three eyes between us. So I got mad and started to punch him, but he ran out and that ended it!"

Ninety-Seven

SPEAKING OF EMPTINESS

A disciple named Subhuti understood the potency of emptiness, the viewpoint that nothing exists except in its relationship of subjectivity and objectivity. One day Subhuti, in a mood of sublime emptiness, was sitting under a tree, and flowers began to fall on him.

"We are praising you for your discourse on emptiness," the celestial devas whispered to Subhuti.

"But I have not spoken of emptiness," said Subhuti.

"You have not spoken of emptiness; we have not heard emptiness," responded the celestial devas. "This is true emptiness."

Ninety-Eight

A HERD OF COWS

A successful farmer had a herd of 250 cows and took great care of them. However, once a tiger ate one of the cows. When the man noticed this, he thought, "I've lost one of my cows, and now my herd is incomplete. What's the point of having all these other cows?" And with that thought, the man drove all the remaining cows off a cliff. He is like a person who, after breaking just one precept of righteousness, thinks, "I've broken one, so I might as well abandon them all."

DEAR SHOVEL

Once lived a very poor farmer whose only food was whatever grew in his small garden. His sole property was one old shovel. The years passed by, and the farmer became weak with age and decided to abandon the physical labour in the garden and instead go into the mountains and lead a life of a hermit. He buried his dear shovel into the ground and went into the mountains hoping to build a little hut there.

Yet, as soon as he left the spot where his shovel was now buried, he got worried and decided to come back and check whether he hid it well. So he did. So the farmer continued on his journey, but again he got overtaken by worries about his shovel. Again and again, he was coming back unable to let go of the only property that fed him for his whole life. Tired and exhausted, the man became angry at himself for not letting go. After all, he was a master of the shovel, not the other way around. So the farmer took the shovel, carried it to the river bank and threw it into the water with all his might. A deep sense of relief filled his heart, and happy with himself, now ready to proceed with the hermit's life, the man shouted, "I won! I won! I won!"

At the same time, on the opposite riverbank, a king was traveling from the neighboring kingdom. Hearing this shouting, the king thought, "I wonder who that man conquered if he screams so loudly? I've conquered many enemies but never yelled like that."

The king then ordered to bring the farmer to him to inquire about his victory.

"O King, You have won thousands of battles and conquered many armies. I humbly conquered myself, but believe me - this is the greatest victory," replied the farmer."

One Hundred

WHERE ARE YOU GOING?

Once a Buddhist monk was walking to another city protected by gates. A soldier guarding the gates interrogated him, "Who are you? Where are you going? Why are you going there?

The monk grew pensive and then asked the soldier, "Could I ask you a question too?"

"What is it?" the soldier wondered with bent brows.

"What do you earn for one week's work?"

"Two baskets of rice," the soldier responded.

"I will bring you four baskets if you ask me these questions every day!"

GOING WITH A FLOW

One day a very old man accidentally fell into the river rapids leading to a high and dangerous waterfall. Onlookers feared for his life. But miraculously, he came out alive and unharmed downstream at the bottom of the falls. When people from his village asked him how he managed to survive, the old man replied, "I accommodated myself to the water, not the water to me. Without thinking, I allowed myself to be shaped by it. Plunging into the swirl, I came out with the swirl. This is how I survived."

BUDDHA'S APPEARANCE

~ᕙ৹ৡৢ৹ᕗ~

One woman lived during the same time as the Buddha. She even lived in the same place where the Buddha taught his discourses, but never did she seek to meet the Buddha, nor want to learn anything from him. Every time she saw him from afar, she would hide or run away. Yet it so happened that one time she didn't have anywhere else to hide. Desperately, the woman closed her face with her hands - and behold! - the Buddha appeared between her fingers.

THE BEST DOCTOR

One person got sick and went to see the doctor. The latter examined him and wrote out a prescription. When the patient returned home, he placed the doctor's portrait in the most conspicuous place, bowed to the portrait three times, lit an incense, took out the prescription, and solemnly began to chant, "Two pills in the morning! Two pills tonight!"

One Hundred and Four

PARABLE OF THE WIDOWER

Once in a small village lived an old man who had a ten-year-old son. He cherished his son more than his own life. One day he left his son at home while he went out on business. When he was gone, bandits came, robbed and burned the entire village. They kidnapped his son. When the man returned home, he found the ashes of a child in his burned house. The father took it to be his son's body and wailed in grief. Because he loved his son so dearly, the man put the ashes in a bag, which he carried everywhere he went.

Several months later, the old man's son managed to escape from the bandits and made his way home. He arrived in the middle of the night and knocked at the door. At that moment, the father was hugging the bag of ashes and weeping. The old man refused to open the door even when the child called out that he was the man's son. The father believed that his own son was dead and that the child knocking at the door was some other child mocking his grief. Finally, his son had no choice but to leave. Thus father and son lost each other forever.

When a person is caught by belief in a doctrine, he loses all his freedom.

ONE SPARK

One evening the Buddha was supposed to preach a sermon on the mountain. A huge crowd awaited him. As it was getting dark, everyone lit their lamps to meet the Buddha. One old woman brought a very small and cheap lamp which the other people ridiculed. The old woman put her lamp next to others despite all the laughter. This woman was so poor that she had to sell everything she owned to buy this little lamp.

Suddenly a stormy wind extinguished all the lights except for the old woman's lamp. As the smallest one, it was protected by the other lamps, and only its flame remained to shine in the dark.

Then Buddha took this little lamp and used it to lit all the other lamps one by one. He then concluded, "As long as there is at least one spark left, hope is not lost."

A CENTIPEDE

Once as a centipede was walking along, when a rabbit called out to her, "Hey, how do you walk so well with your legs all going in different directions simultaneously? And yet, you don't get tangled up and can walk so smoothly without stumbling?"

The centipede listened carefully to what the rabbit said and agreed that it was incredible that she could walk so smoothly. Thinking this, the centipede looked down at her legs and immediately tripped and fell over, unable to take even a single step forward any longer.

One Hundred and Seven

SEARCHING FOR GOD

A hermit was meditating by a river when a young man addressed him.

"Master, I wish to become your disciple," said the young man.

"Why?" asked the hermit.

The young man thought for a moment and replied, "Because I want to find God."

The hermit jumped up, grabbed the young man by the scruff of his neck, dragged him into the river, and plunged his head underwater. After holding him there for a minute, with him kicking and struggling to free himself, the hermit finally pulled him up out of the river. The young man coughed up water and gasped to get his breath. When he eventually quieted down, the hermit spoke, "Tell me, what did you want most of all when you were underwater."

"Air!" the man exclaimed.

"Very well," said the hermit. "Go home and come back to me when you want God as much as you just wanted air."

One Hundred and Eight

A SIGNIFICANT CAT

Once when a famous spiritual teacher and his disciples began their evening meditation, the cat who lived in the monastery made such a loud noise that distracted them. So the teacher ordered that the cat be tied up during the evening practice. Years later, when the teacher died, the cat continued to be tied up during the meditation session. And when the cat eventually died, another cat was brought to the monastery and tied up. Centuries later, learned descendants of the spiritual teacher wrote scholarly treatises about the religious significance of tying up a cat for meditation practice.

Made in United States
Troutdale, OR
12/13/2023